THE ASTROLABE, an instrument developed by the Greeks, is the symbol for JUNIOR WORLD EXPLORERS. At the time of Columbus, sailors used the astrolabe to chart a ship's course. The arm across the circle could be moved to line up with the sun or a star. Using the number indicated by the pointer, a sailor could tell his approximate location on the sea. Although the astrolabe was not completely accurate, it helped many early explorers in their efforts to conquer the unknown.

Junior World Explorers

John Smith

by Charles P. Graves
illustrated by Al Fiorentino

Chelsea Juniors
A division of Chelsea House Publishers
New York ▪ Philadelphia

To Betty Braxton, another venturesome Virginian

Cover Illustration: Gil Ashby

First Chelsea House edition 1991

1 3 5 7 9 8 6 4 2

ISBN   0-7910-1499-1

Contents

1

The Spanish Armada

John Smith stood by his family's farm-house near Willoughby, England. Night had just fallen and he was staring across the marshes toward the sea.

Suddenly a bonfire lit the eastern sky. This was followed by another blaze a few miles away and then another. Soon a whole chain of bonfires stretched across the land.

John Smith gazed at the fires with growing excitement. He was only eight, but he knew what the fires meant. They were a signal.

"The Armada!" John screamed as he ran toward his house. "Father, the Spanish Armada is coming!"

The Armada was a fleet of 132 ships that King Philip of Spain was sending to conquer England. The year was 1588. At that time Spain was the most powerful nation in the world.

"The Armada is coming!" John Smith shouted again as he raced toward his house.

The front door flew open. John's father and mother and his younger brother, Francis, dashed outside.

Mr. Smith took one look at the bonfires. "It's the Armada all right."

"Should I hide the children?" Mrs. Smith asked. The baby, Alice, was asleep in the house.

"The Armada is probably still a long way from here," Mr. Smith said. "The signal means it has been sighted off southern England."

"Sir Francis Drake won't let the Spanish land without a fight," John cried. "I'm sure of that!"

Francis Drake was a hero to English schoolboys. Just eight years before, in 1580, he had been the first Englishman to complete a voyage around the world.

Drake had also captured Spanish ships and destroyed some Spanish settlements in America. Now he was trying to defend England from the Armada.

"I wish I could sail with Sir Francis Drake," John said.

"It's time you and Francis *Smith* sailed right to bed," Mrs. Smith said. "Tomorrow is a school day."

The next morning John and Francis did their chores. They milked the cows and fed the chickens.

Then the boys walked the four miles to school at Alford. The teacher had a hard time keeping the children quiet that day. All they could think about was the Armada. England might be invaded at any minute.

News traveled slowly then. Day after day went by and there was no word.

"What do you think is happening?" Francis asked John.

"England must be winning," John said. "If the Spaniards had landed we would know by now."

At last news started to trickle in. The

English had outfought the Armada. Many Spanish ships had been sunk. Some that escaped were wrecked in a storm before they could reach Spain.

"Isn't it wonderful that the battle is over?" Mr. Smith said that night.

John looked glum. "I'm not so sure."

"Why not?"

"I wanted to fight with Sir Francis Drake and have lots of adventures. There probably won't be any adventures left when I grow up."

Mr. Smith laughed. "Don't worry about that, son. There'll always be adventures for brave men. Besides, you don't need a war to have adventures. Remember that."

2

Man Overboard!

"Who knows what England's victory means?" asked John's schoolteacher. John raised his hand.

"All right, Master Smith."

"It means the English are better sailors than the Spanish."

The teacher smiled. "It means more than that. It means that England, not Spain, will soon rule the seas. Now perhaps England can build colonies in America."

England had tried to start colonies in the past, but each attempt had failed. Spain was glad they had. She had colonies already and wanted to keep America to herself.

The English did not send colonists to America right away, but they did gain control of the seas. As time went on, England grew more and more powerful.

John Smith grew tall and powerful too. He did some of the hardest work on his father's farm.

"I don't mind working," John often said. "But I don't like farming."

"It's a good life, son," Mr. Smith said.

"It's too dull for me, Father."

"Are you still dreaming about those adventures? Try to forget them. Your mother and I need you on the farm. There's adventure enough right here."

John disagreed, but there was little he could say. Someday . . . John kept his dreams.

When John was about sixteen his father died. His mother married again and moved away from the farm. At last his chance had come! John was free to leave.

But where could he find adventure? Holland! He knew the Dutch were trying to gain their freedom from Spain. Many Englishmen were helping them fight.

John went to Holland and fought for three years. He learned to take orders and to march many miles without food. He became a good marksman.

Sometimes the Dutch used fireworks against the Spanish. John became an expert at making fireworks and setting them off.

When John returned to England he was a hardened soldier—and a man.

"Tell us some war stories, John," his friends in Willoughby begged.

John told some of his adventures, but his friends kept asking for more. John grew tired of seeing people. He wanted to be alone to plan his future.

He built a hut by a brook in the forest nearby. He bought a horse and rode it every day. Soon he was an excellent horseman. He shot deer for meat and improved his marksmanship.

He also read books on the art of war. A chapter about signaling with lights fascinated him.

John was living an easy life. "Too easy," he said to himself. "I'm ready for more adventures."

John heard that the Turks had invaded

Hungary, a country in eastern Europe. The Hungarians needed brave men to help them fight. John decided to help.

Hungary was a long way from England. John went to France and boarded a ship that was sailing to Italy. From there he planned to go to Hungary by land.

Soon after the ship left France, a French passenger stepped up to John.

"All Englishmen are pirates!" the Frenchman sneered.

Blood rushed to John's face. "Take that back!"

As John raised his fists, more of the Frenchmen crowded around him. "We don't want any Englishmen on this ship," one of them cried. "The English bring bad luck."

"Throw him overboard!" another man shouted.

The Frenchmen rushed at John. He tried to fight them off but there were too many. Two of the men knocked him down. Others grabbed his arms and legs. They threw him over the side of the ship and he splashed into the water. The ship sailed on.

John wasn't a good swimmer, but he had a lot of courage. He saw an island in the distance and started swimming toward it.

The sea was rough. Waves beat against his face. He was breathing so hard that his lungs hurt. "I won't give up!" he said to himself. "I can make it if I try hard enough."

Slowly John got closer to the island. When his strength was almost gone he tried to reach bottom. His toes just touched the sand. He staggered ashore.

John tried to find a house, but the island was deserted. He lay down under a tree and went to sleep.

The next morning John searched for something to eat. He came to a cove and saw two ships anchored there.

John called and waved. Finally one of the ships sent a small boat ashore for him. The ship was going to Egypt. That was a long way from Hungary, but John thought it would be an exciting trip.

The ship sailed across the Mediterranean Sea and along the coast of Africa. It unloaded its cargo in Egypt and then sailed to Italy. John left the ship in Italy and slowly made his way to Hungary. At last he had reached his destination!

3

Captain Smith

John met an officer in the Hungarian army named Ebersbaught.

"I want to fight for Hungary," John said.

"Have you had military experience?" Ebersbaught asked.

John told him that he had fought the Spanish in Holland and that he had studied the art of war in books. "I learned how to send secret messages—without a messenger," he added.

Ebersbaught looked interested. "Tell me about it."

"Suppose you were surrounded by the enemy," John began. "No messenger could get through to you. Still, I could send you a secret message."

"How?"

"By signaling with torchlights," John replied.

"Explain it, young man," Ebersbaught ordered.

John got a piece of paper and wrote down the code. "You use one light to send the letters in the first part of the alphabet. For instance, to signal 'a' you show one light one time. To signal 'b' you show one light twice. One light three times means 'c,' four times 'd' and so on."

"What about the second part of the alphabet?" Ebersbaught asked.

"The letters are sent the same way except that two lights are used for each letter. Two lights once mean 'm,' two lights twice mean 'n' and so on."

"I understand. But how does the receiver know when a word ends?"

"The sender shows three lights at once."

"That's a clever code," Ebersbaught said. "If I'm ever surrounded by Turks I hope you'll be nearby."

Ebersbaught sent John to a general named Kisell. The general put John in his army as an artilleryman.

A short time later Kisell heard that Ebersbaught and his soldiers were trapped in the town of Oberlimbach. They were surrounded by 20,000 Turks.

Kisell marched to Oberlimbach to try to rescue Ebersbaught's army. Kisell had only 10,000 men. The Turks outnumbered him two to one.

John Smith went to Kisell's tent. "Sir, I believe we can trick the Turks. I will send a message to Ebersbaught."

"Nonsense!" Kisell snorted. "He is trapped. No messenger can get through."

"Light can go anywhere," John said. "I will send a message by torchlight." He told Kisell about the secret code.

John outlined his plan to trick the Turks. He would make some fireworks that looked like men firing guns. He would set them off on Thursday night. The Turks would think they were being attacked. They would rush to counter-attack, leaving the gates unguarded.

When Ebersbaught heard the fireworks he would lead his soldiers through the gates and attack the Turks from the

rear. Kisell would attack from the side.

Kisell approved the plan. That night John climbed a hill and lit his torches. He sent a message to Ebersbaught. Ebersbaught flashed a message back saying that he understood.

John made his fireworks. On Thursday night he lit the fuses. The "fighting men" exploded noisily in all directions.

To the Turks the fireworks looked like a great army charging with guns firing.

24

They turned to fight this imaginary army.

At the same time Ebersbaught led his soldiers through the gates. Kisell's army attacked too. ST. GABRIEL SCHOOL

The Turks were caught in a trap. It was a great victory for the Hungarians. John Smith had made the victory possible.

Kisell sent for him. "You are a fine soldier," he said. "I'm going to promote you to captain. You will be in command of 250 horsemen."

4

Slave

Smith and his horsemen rode with the Hungarian army to Szekesfehervar which was held by the Turks. There was a high wall around the city.

The Turks stayed behind the wall, and the Hungarians could not shoot them. Once again Smith called on his knowledge of fireworks.

He got some pots and filled them with gunpowder, bullets and pitch. The pitch was lighted and the pots thrown over the wall. The gunpowder exploded and the bullets flew in all directions. Many Turkish soldiers were killed. Smith called his pots "fiery dragons."

After Szekesfehervar was captured the Hungarians attacked still another city. Even with "fiery dragons" they could not capture it.

During a lull in the fighting, some Turks climbed onto the city wall and hurled insults at Captain Smith and his men. One of the Turks challenged one of Smith's men to single combat. Smith himself accepted the challenge.

The Turk's name was Turbashaw. He rode out of the city on a beautiful horse. A pair of eagle wings was fixed to his shoulders. The wings were decorated with silver, gold and precious stones.

Captain Smith mounted his own horse and went to meet Turbashaw. At a signal the two horsemen galloped toward each other, holding their lances before them.

"Clang!" Smith's lance hit the Turk on the chest. It pierced his armor. Turbashaw fell to the ground.

Two other Turks challenged Smith and he defeated them both. "Nobody will ever beat me," he bragged.

Smith spoke too soon. In the next big battle he was badly wounded. His comrades had to retreat and leave him moaning on the battlefield.

Soon he heard some Turkish soldiers coming toward him. He tried to play dead, but one of the Turks saw that he was still breathing.

"This one is still alive!" the Turk cried. "Let's finish him off." He raised his sword, ready to run it through Smith's body.

"Wait!" another Turkish soldier said. "He looks strong. If we sold him as a slave we could get a high price."

The Turkish soldiers took Smith to their camp and nursed him back to health. Then they sold him as a slave. The man who bought Smith sent him to a young woman in Constantinople.

Her name was Charatza. She liked Smith, but she kept him only a short time. She sent him to live with her brother.

"He will take good care of you," she told Smith. But she didn't know her brother well. He hated Smith. He put an iron ring around Smith's neck so that everyone would know he was a slave. He made him wear a rough hair shirt.

Smith was beaten regularly and made to work long hours. He dreamed of escape, but there was little chance of that.

One day Smith was in a field threshing grain with a big, wooden flail. Charatza's brother came to watch him. The two men were alone.

"You're not working hard enough," he said to Smith. He pulled a rawhide whip from his belt. "This will teach you how to work!" He lifted the whip above his head. With all his might he brought it down on Smith's back.

The pain was awful. Smith became so angry that he lost his head. He tightened his grip on the wooden flail and turned on his tormentor. As Charatza's brother raised his whip to strike again, Smith

swung the flail against his head. The man fell to the ground dead.

This was Smith's chance to escape. Quickly he took off his own rough clothes and put on those of the dead man.

Now his hair shirt would not give him away as an escaped slave. But the iron ring was still around his neck.

Smith hid in the woods until it was dark. Then he traveled as far as he could before dawn. By hiding in the day-time and traveling at night he finally reached Russia.

The Russians didn't like the Turks. They agreed to help Smith. They removed the iron ring from his neck.

After a long journey Smith finally reached England in 1604. He was only 24 years old, but he had already had a lifetime of adventures.

5

America

The greatest adventure of all still lay ahead for John Smith. England was ready to try to build colonies in North America.

James I was now King of England. He gave permission for two companies of businessmen to form colonies. They were the London Company and the Plymouth Company.

England claimed all of North America between Florida and Canada. She called the whole country Virginia. The London Company was planning an expedition to the southern part. The Plymouth Company would try to plant a colony in the north.

John Smith went to see the leaders of the London Company. "I've had a great deal of experience traveling and fighting," he said. "You need a man like me to help you start your colony in America."

"We hope there won't be any fighting," a member of the London Company said. "We want our colonists to find gold and silver."

"Are you sure there is gold and silver in Virginia?" Smith asked.

"The Spanish found it in South America," a man said. "We think it's in Virginia too." He went on to tell Smith the company's other plans. The business-men wanted to find a waterway to the Pacific Ocean. This shortcut would make it easy for the English to trade with China and the rich East Indies. The owners also wanted the colony to send home furs, lumber and other goods.

John Smith was excited when the London Company hired him. He thought of his childhood hero, Sir Francis Drake. "Now I can help England the way Drake did," he said to himself.

Smith helped make preparations for the voyage. Three small ships were chosen: the *Susan Constant*, the *Goodspeed* and the *Discovery*. The ships were loaded with food, tools, weapons and other supplies.

Late in December, 1606, the three ships sailed with more than 100 men. Smith

looked at the men on his ship doubtfully. Most of them were "gentlemen" who had never done any real work in their lives. They hoped to find gold in Virginia and become rich quickly.

John Smith knew the expedition needed farmers, carpenters, bricklayers and blacksmiths. Hardworking laborers would be able to make homes in the wilderness.

Captain Christopher Newport was in charge of the men on the voyage across the ocean. No one aboard the ships knew who the leaders would be in America. The London Company had kept that secret. The names of the leaders were in a sealed box on the *Susan Constant.*

"Do not open the box until you reach Virginia," Captain Newport had been told.

Smith felt sure he would be a leader.

Few of the "fine gentlemen" knew any-thing practical. Smith found himself telling them what to do.

This made him unpopular. Someone told Newport that Smith was planning a mutiny. This was not true, but Newport believed it. He had Smith arrested and confined below decks.

It was a long voyage. Finally, on April 26, 1607, they sighted a cape in Virginia. They named it Cape Henry after the older son of King James.

Smith was allowed on deck. He gazed at Virginia for the first time. The white sand beach sparkled in the sunshine. Beyond the beach a forest stretched as far as he could see.

Before the men could decide on a place for a settlement they had to find out who their leaders would be. Captain Newport

broke open the sealed box and read the paper inside.

"The following men will be our leaders and make up our governing council," he said. "Besides myself the members of the council will be Edward Wingfield, George Kendall, John Martin, John Ratcliffe, Bartholomew Gosnold and"—he paused for a moment—"John Smith."

Smith stepped forward, a smile on his face.

"Not you, Smith," Newport said. "You're still under arrest."

Smith's anger flared, for he knew he was innocent. But he kept his temper.

The London Company had told the men to build their town some distance up a river. They wanted it to be safe from attack by Spanish ships.

On May 13, the ships sailed up a broad

river which they named the James, after the king. They found a peninsula that had tall trees growing right down to the river's edge. They decided to build their town on the peninsula. They tied the ships to the trees and started unloading their supplies.

The land was low and marshy. It was certainly not a healthy place to build a town. But John Smith saw that it would

be easy to defend the peninsula against attacks by Indians. That was a big advantage.

The council named their settlement "Jamestown." Smith was set to work with the other men. They cut down trees to make room for their tents.

Later Smith started clearing land for a garden. "I'm glad now that my father taught me how to farm," he thought.

Most of the men didn't want to help Smith. They wanted to start hunting gold and silver at once.

Smith was furious. "You must help me!" he cried. "Our supplies won't last forever. We need food and shelter—not gold! England's other colonies in America failed. Jamestown must be a permanent settlement."

The men grumbled, but the leaders realized Smith was right. This was the wilderness. They were thousands of miles from England.

Although Smith was still officially under arrest he was allowed to speak his mind and to move about freely. Every man was needed in the fight for survival.

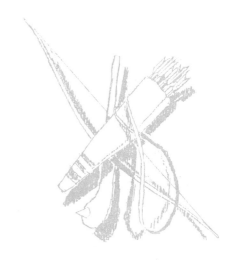

6

Indians

One morning Captain Smith and some other men were chopping down trees at the edge of the settlement. Suddenly, Smith heard voices. He turned around and saw at least 100 Indians coming across the marshes.

The Indians were almost naked. Their heads were decorated with feathers and fur and they carried war clubs.

At first the Indians seemed friendly. They had never seen white men before, and they stared in wonder at the English.

The Indians came closer. One of them darted forward and grabbed a hatchet from one of the men. The Englishman dashed after the Indian. He could not afford to lose such a valuable tool. As he reached for his hatchet another Indian leaped forward and knocked him down.

Captain Smith and the other Englishmen dropped their hatchets and picked up their guns. They fired over the heads of the Indians.

The Indians had never heard gunfire before. They fled in terror.

John Smith was afraid they might return. He wanted to build a wall around Jamestown and train the men to fight.

Instead, he was sent with an exploring

party up the James River in a small boat called a shallop.

Smith thoroughly enjoyed the trip. "We're the first Englishmen ever to see this beautiful country," he said to his companions.

One morning the explorers met some friendly Indians in a canoe. Smith used sign language to talk to them. But he knew it was important for an explorer to be able to speak the natives' language. He started learning Indian words.

An Indian named Navirans helped him. Smith taught Navirans how to use pen and ink. The Indian drew a map of the river. The map was a big help to Smith.

The explorers went on up the river until they came to a waterfall. They could go no farther in the shallop, so they returned to Jamestown.

"Indians attacked us while you were away," one of the men at Jamestown told Smith. "They killed a boy and wounded sixteen men."

"Where were your guns?" Smith asked.

"We didn't have them handy."

Smith shook his head. "You should be ready to fight at all times," he said. Smith learned that all the men at Jamestown might have been killed if the sailors on one of the ships had not fired a cannon. The tremendous roar scared the Indians away.

There was more on Smith's mind than Indians. He was still under arrest for mutiny. He demanded a trial to prove his innocence.

At the trial Smith was found not guilty. He took his place on the council which governed Jamestown.

Captain Smith tried to set a good example by working harder than any other man in the colony. He helped plan and build a log fort and helped the men build houses. Smith knew the settlers must have shelters if they were to survive the winter ahead. Many had already died of disease and exposure. The men began to respect Smith's ability.

One day Smith went down to the river's edge to say good-bye to Captain Newport. He was sailing back to England.

"I'll be back with more supplies as soon as possible," Newport promised.

"That may not be soon enough," Smith thought. He realized that Captain Newport might be shipwrecked. He might never return.

Smith was afraid the settlers would starve during the winter unless they got

more food and stored it at Jamestown. The men had planted gardens, but the harvest would be small.

Smith decided to take a boat and visit an Indian village. He knew the Indians would trade corn, fish and meat for some of the English tools and trinkets.

"I hate to part with the tools," Smith said, "but our people must have food."

Smith was a good trader. He returned to Jamestown with his boat full of food. It wasn't enough to last through the winter, but it would help.

Most of the men at Jamestown became discouraged. They wanted to try to sail back to England in one of the small boats.

"No," Smith said firmly. "We won't give up now! We're in Virginia to stay!"

Ambush!

In December, Smith and a party of men went on another exploring trip. They took a barge up the James River and turned into the Chickahominy.

Smith was determined to go to the source of the Chickahominy. "Perhaps it flows out of a lake," he thought. "Perhaps there is another river, on the other side of the lake, that flows into the Pacific Ocean."

The farther up the river they went, the shallower it became. Finally the barge could go no farther.

Smith saw two friendly Indians in a canoe. He knew that a canoe would float in just a few inches of water. Smith offered the Indians some presents if they would paddle him on up the stream.

The Indians agreed. Smith and two other Englishmen, John Robinson and Thomas Emry, climbed into the canoe.

After they had gone about a dozen miles the river got very narrow. Smith decided to go ashore and explore the land.

He turned to Robinson and Emry, "I'll take one Indian with me for a guide. You and the other Indian stay here. Do not leave the canoe. If any unfriendly Indians show up, fire a warning shot. I'll hear it and come back to help."

Smith and his guide disappeared in the forest. When they had been gone about fifteen minutes they heard a loud cry and some Indian yells. But they heard no shot.

"Perhaps Robinson and Emry were surprised," Smith thought. "Maybe they didn't have time to fire a gun."

He and his guide started back toward the canoe. They'd taken only a few steps when an arrow whistled through the air. It hit Smith's thigh. Fortunately it struck at an angle and didn't do much damage.

Smith whirled about. He saw two Indians with drawn bows. He whipped out his pistol and fired at them. He missed, but the Indians raced away.

More Indians appeared and started shooting arrows. Smith and his guide were surrounded.

Smith gripped his pistol firmly. He

tried to break through the ring of Indians. But he could not watch the Indians and also watch where he was stepping. Suddenly, Smith and his guide fell into a mudhole.

Captain Smith held the Indians at bay with his pistol. But it was a cold winter day, and he was soaking wet. He was afraid he might freeze to death in the mudhole. He had to surrender.

First he let his pistol sink out of sight in the mud. He did not want the Indians to have it.

When they saw he had no pistol the Indians grabbed Smith. They took him back to the riverbank and showed him the dead bodies of Robinson and Emry. The two men had disobeyed Smith's orders. They had come ashore and built a fire.

"If they had stayed in the canoe they would still be alive," Smith thought.

An Indian chief came up to Smith. He pointed to his chest and said "Opechancanough." Smith knew this was Chief Opechancanough, the brother of Chief Powhatan. Powhatan was the most powerful chief in that part of Virginia.

Smith stared into Opechancanough's dark eyes. He was certainly ferocious looking.

"I must find a present for him," Smith thought. He dug his hand into one of his pockets. His fingers closed around a small compass.

"Maybe he'll like this," Smith thought hopefully.

Opechancanough was delighted with the compass. Smith tried to show him how to use it.

Suddenly Opechancanough grew tired of his toy. He and the other Indians tied Smith to a tree. Some of the braves put arrows in their bowstrings. It looked like the end of Captain Smith.

Opechancanough's mood changed again. He told the braves not to shoot. Then he untied Smith and took him to an Indian village named Orapaks.

The Indians at Orapaks formed a circle around Smith and started a war dance. They screamed wildly and waved their tomahawks at Smith. He felt sure they would kill him.

The dance stopped as quickly as it had begun. Some squaws brought Smith a lot of food. For the moment he seemed safe.

8

Pocahontas

The Indians took Smith to another village named Werowocomoco. This was where Chief Powhatan lived.

Smith was led into a long house. Powhatan sat on a high seat piled with mats. Smith saw that he had gray hair and a stern expression. He wore a robe of animal skins. Pearls hung from his neck.

Many braves and squaws sat on each side of Powhatan. There was a group of children nearby.

The braves whooped when Smith arrived. But he was not afraid of their screeches now. He had heard them too often.

The Indians brought water for him to wash his hands. They gave him some feathers to use as a towel. Then they gave him some food.

"These are friendly Indians," Smith
thought.

Powhatan fastened his eyes on Smith.
He spoke in the Indian language which
Smith now knew fairly well.

"Why have you English come to my
country?" Powhatan asked.

That was a hard question. Smith knew
that the Indians thought they owned all
the land in Virginia. The English thought
it belonged to them. An explorer in an

English ship had discovered Virginia many years before. Smith was afraid to tell Powhatan that the English planned to stay in Virginia.

"A Spanish ship chased us to Virginia," Smith said. "We escaped by sailing up the river. We will leave soon."

Powhatan did not believe him. He ordered his braves to bring two big stones and place them at his feet. When that was done the braves grabbed Smith and forced his head against the stones. The Indians then picked up their clubs.

It was clear that the Indians planned to kill Smith. He closed his eyes and waited for the blows.

Just then a thirteen-year-old girl ran toward Smith. The Indians gasped when they saw her. She was Powhatan's daughter, Pocahontas.

The Indian girl darted between the raised clubs of the braves and laid her head against Smith's. If the braves killed Smith they would have to kill her too.

Powhatan raised his hand and ordered the Indians to lower their clubs.

Pocahontas looked up. "Please, Father," she begged, "let the Englishman live. He is a brave man and has done no wrong."

Powhatan loved his daughter. He agreed not to kill Smith. He looked at the Englishman.

"In return for your life," he said, "you must give us presents. I want bells and beads for Pocahontas and guns and a grindstone for me."

Smith promised to send Powhatan the gifts as soon as he reached Jamestown.

Then he turned to Pocahontas. "Thank you," he said. "You have saved my life."

Pocahontas gave him a shy smile. When Smith left for Jamestown she told him that she would like to visit the settlement someday.

Powhatan sent twelve braves with Smith. He ordered them to bring back the presents Smith had promised.

Smith didn't want Powhatan to have guns. He was afraid the Indians might use them to kill the English. So he tricked the braves when they reached Jamestown. He gave them two giant cannons. Each one weighed more than two tons. The Indians could not lift them.

"I have kept my promise," Smith said. He gave the Indian braves a grindstone for Powhatan and some beads and bells for Pocahontas.

President

Soon there was more trouble with the Indians. They started sneaking into Jamestown to steal tools and weapons.

One day Smith captured four Indians inside the town gates. He said he would not let them go until all the stolen goods were returned.

Powhatan sent Pocahontas to ask Smith to free the Indians. Smith was glad to see her.

"What can I do for you?" he asked.

"Let the Indians go free."

Smith didn't hesitate. He let Pocahontas take the four Indians back to Powhatan.

Pocahontas returned to Jamestown many times. She brought food to trade. She began to learn English.

Other Indians came to Jamestown too. They would not trade with anyone except Smith. They felt that they could trust him. If it hadn't been for Smith many colonists would have starved.

More settlers were coming to Jamestown from England. But they were not the kind of men the settlement needed. They were not interested in building houses or farming. They only wanted to find gold.

Hard work was what it took to build a colony in the wilderness. Smith could not respect men who wouldn't work.

"We don't need gold," he said. "You can't eat gold. We need food."

Whenever he could, Smith went on trading and exploring trips. He had come to love Virginia. He thought the forests and rivers were beautiful.

Once he went to the Chesapeake Bay and turned north. He entered the Potomac River and went as far as Great Falls, near the present site of Washington, D.C.

On his way back, he saw schools of fish so thick that he could spear them with his sword. Once he speared a stingray. When he tried to take it off his sword the fish drove its stinger deep into Smith's arm. It was extremely painful. Later, however, Smith ate some of the stingray for supper.

Smith returned to Jamestown. The

members of the council had come to realize that he was the most able man in the colony. They elected him president.

Before taking office Smith wanted to go exploring again. This time he was determined to go to the northern end of Chesapeake Bay. When he reached it he explored the Susquehanna River. Rocks, blocking the way, forced him back.

On all his explorations Smith made careful notes of the landmarks, rivers and bays. He learned as much as he could about the climate, soil, trees, plants and wild animals. He also made maps of the areas he saw. He knew that this information would be valuable to others who might want to settle in America.

Smith became Jamestown's president on September 10, 1608. He was the best president the little settlement ever had.

He trained the men to fight. He had target practice. "We never know," he said, "when friendly Indians may become our enemies."

He also made lazy men work. "If you won't work," he said, "you won't eat."

The men worked and Jamestown became stronger. It was now a year and a half since the settlement was founded. A number of houses had been built and streets laid out. The fields were green with crops.

No man worked harder than Captain Smith. He even worked at night. He wrote a history of Jamestown and drew a map of Virginia. He sent these back to England. Many Englishmen became interested in coming to Jamestown after they had read his history.

10

Powhatan's Plot

Toward the end of 1608, there was another food shortage in Jamestown. Smith asked Powhatan for corn.

"No," the chief said. "I will not help you any more. I want you to leave my country."

Powhatan hoped he could starve out the Englishmen. But Captain Smith would not give up.

"I'll find some way to get more food," he vowed.

A short time later Powhatan sent word to Jamestown that he wanted some Englishmen to help him build a house. Smith suspected that this was a trick. But he thought he might be able to outwit Powhatan and get corn.

He sent some carpenters by land to Werowocomoco. Smith and some other men went by boat. They hoped to fill the boat with Indian corn.

The first night, Smith and his men came ashore and made camp. It was terribly cold, and the fire warmed them.

While Smith relaxed by the fire, an Indian slipped out of the forest and stood before him.

"Beware of Powhatan!" the Indian whispered.

"He sent for us," Smith said. "Is it a trick?"

"Powhatan plans to cut your throat," the Indian warned. "He thinks the English would go home if you were dead."

"Thank you for warning me."

Smith didn't think of turning back, but he was glad he had been warned.

The next day he reached Werowocomoco and saw Powhatan at once. "I want to buy some corn," Smith began.

"I will trade corn for guns and swords," Powhatan said.

"I have no guns or swords to spare," Smith replied. "I will give you beads."

"I do not trust you," Powhatan said. "You say you come to trade. But many Indians think you plan to steal our country."

"I am your friend," Smith said. "I only want to trade."

"Prove you are my friend," the chief

said. "Leave your guns in your boat. Then I will trade."

Smith knew the Indians might kill the English if they were unarmed.

"We can't leave our guns today," he answered. "We'll do it tomorrow."

At first Powhatan seemed satisfied. The two men began to trade. Slowly, a big hill of corn grew at Smith's feet. Then suddenly Powhatan ran off into the woods.

A group of Indians surrounded Smith. Many of them had stone knives.

Holding their guns in front of them, Smith and his men forced the Indians back. They broke through the circle and ran to their boat.

Other Indians appeared carrying baskets filled with the corn Smith had left behind.

One of the Indians said, "You carry the baskets now."

Smith knew it was another trick. If the Englishmen were to pick up the baskets, they would first have to lay down their guns. The Indians would grab the guns and shoot them.

Captain Smith aimed his gun at one of the Indians. "Put that corn on our boat!" he ordered.

The Indians were afraid of Smith's gun. They put the corn on the boat, and Smith and his men prepared to leave. The tide was low and the boat stuck in the mud. It was too cold to stay on the river. The Englishmen went to an Indian hut to keep warm.

There was a soft knock. Smith looked up. It was Pocahontas.

"Sh-h," the Indian girl whispered. "You are in great danger. My father is going to entertain you with food and dancing.

While you're enjoying yourself he plans to kill you. You must leave at once."

"Thank you, Pocahontas," Smith said. "We are grateful. Let me give you something as a reward."

"No!" the girl cried. "If my father saw the present he would know I warned you."

Pocahontas slipped away. Smith and his men stayed awake until the tide came in. Then they escaped from Werowocomoco.

Back at Jamestown, Smith learned that the other members of the council had died while he was away. Now he alone governed the colony. He ruled with a strong hand.

The colony began to produce such things as tar, pitch, soap ashes, boards and glass. These products were sent to to England. Jamestown was beginning to pay its way.

11

England Again

The English had now been in America for more than two years. But Jamestown was the only settlement.

Smith thought the colony would be stronger if other towns were built. He sent one group of men up the river and another group down the river to start towns.

He made all the men work hard. Many of them grumbled. Some even wrote letters about him to the London Company in England. The letters did not tell the truth. One letter even said that Smith was planning to marry Pocahontas and make himself King of Virginia.

In September Smith went up the river to see how the men at the new settlement were getting along. He was angry with what he saw. The men had settled on land that would be flooded in heavy rains. They had stolen corn from the Indians and had fought with them.

Smith had the settlement moved to high ground and then started back to Jamestown. He fell asleep in the boat. His powder bag hung from his belt.

One of his companions was smoking a pipe. A spark flew from the pipe and settled on Smith's powder bag. There was a loud explosion, and Smith's clothes caught fire.

Smith woke and jumped overboard to put out the fire. He was in such pain that he almost drowned. The men in the boat pulled him aboard.

His burns were serious. When he reached Jamestown, he found that there was no medicine to help him.

"You must take the next ship back to England," one of his friends said. "You'll get better care there."

Smith hated to leave. But he knew it was the right thing to do. Jamestown was strong enough now to live without him.

He stood on the deck of his ship and watched Jamestown fade from sight. The sea gulls swooped and cried overhead as if they were sorry to see him leave.

"Maybe Jamestown is not a large settlement," Smith thought, "but at least it's a start. It's a seed. And before any tree can grow, a seed must be planted." He felt sure that someday soon many Englishmen would make their homes in America.

In England Smith had his burns treated. Then he asked the London Company to send him back to Virginia. But the leaders of the Company would not hire him again. They believed the untrue stories told by Smith's enemies.

Smith thought of America all the time. He wrote books about it. He praised the mild Virginia climate, the fertile soil and the rivers that made transportation so easy. Many people who read his books decided to become colonists.

Whenever he could, Smith talked to

sailors who had returned from Virginia. He heard about the dreadful winter of 1610. The food in Jamestown gave out and many people starved to death.

Perhaps if Smith had been there he could have prevented the "starving time."

One day Smith had news of Pocahontas. "She married an Englishman named John Rolfe," a sailor told him. "They are growing that Indian weed—tobacco."

"Ugh!" Smith said. "I have no love for tobacco. King James says it is hateful to the nose, harmful to the brain and dangerous to the lungs. If it hadn't been for a pipe smoker I would still be in Virginia."

Smith was remembering the burns that had sent him back to England.

12

Admiral of New England

In 1614, almost five years after he returned to England, Smith sailed for America again. Some London merchants put him in charge of an expedition that was sailing to what was then called Northern Virginia.

The merchants told Smith to bring back whale oil, gold and copper. "If you find none of these," one of the merchants said, "bring us fish and furs."

One of the passengers on Smith's ship was a young Indian named Squanto. He had been brought to England by fishermen. Squanto had enjoyed life there and had learned English. But now he wanted to return to his own people.

There were two ships in the expedition. After a voyage of six weeks the ships anchored by an island off the coast of Maine. The men started hunting for whales. But they had no experience in whaling. All the whales got away.

The men went ashore and searched for gold and copper, but they didn't find any. Smith felt sure there was no gold in that part of America.

They started trapping and fishing. "I'm not a trapper or a fisherman," Smith said. "I'm an explorer."

So Smith and eight men went exploring

in a small boat. This was the work Smith loved best.

They explored and mapped the rocky coast, the islands, harbors and rivers. Smith knew that this beautiful country could be tamed by English settlers.

The best land of all, he thought, was that which the Indians called Massachusetts. There were plenty of fish in the waters, animals on land, trees for building houses and pure water to drink. Smith said that Massachusetts was the *"Paradise of all those parts."*

The Indians were friendly. It would be a fine place for a colony.

On the return trip to England, Smith made a map of the coast he had explored. He called the northern part of Virginia *New England.*

People were excited by John Smith's

description of New England. He was given a new ship so he could start a colony there. Again he set sail.

In the Atlantic he met with pirates and was forced to return to England. Smith was bitterly disappointed, but at least something came out of the voyage. On shipboard he wrote a book called *A Description of New England.*

He decided to print the map he'd made earlier with the book. He asked Prince Charles, King James' younger son, to name some of the places on the map.

The Prince named a river in Massachusetts after himself. This is the Charles River which flows into Boston harbor today.

When the map was printed Smith was given a new title. *Admiral of New England* appears by his name.

The map and the book helped the Pilgrims when they sailed to America in 1620. They built their settlement at a place named on Smith's map. It was Plymouth, Massachusetts.

Smith never did go back to America. But he saw his favorite American friend once again. Pocahontas came to England with her husband.

"I will always call you *father*," she told Smith, "and you must call me *child*."

Smith died in 1631. Before he died he learned that the colonies in Virginia and New England were thriving.

Captain Smith had never married. Once a stranger asked, "Have you any children?"

"I have two children," John Smith said proudly, "Virginia and New England are my children."